GENTLEMEN, THIS IS A FOOTBALL

GENTLEMEN,

Compiled by ERIC ZWEIG

FOOTBALL'S BEST
QUOTES AND QUIPS

THIS IS A
FOOTBALL

FIREFLY BOOKS

A FIREFLY BOOK

Published by Firefly Books Ltd. 2006

First printing

PUBLISHER CATALOGING-IN-PUBLICATION DATA (U.S.)
Gentlemen, this is a football : football's best quotes and quips / compiled by Eric Zweig.
[176] p. : photos. (chiefly col.) ; cm.
Includes index.
ISBN-13: 978-1-55407-228-6 (pbk.)
ISBN-10: 1-55407-228-X (pbk.)
1. Football — United States — Quotations, maxims, etc. I. Zweig, Eric.
II. Title.
796.332 dc22 GV950.5G46 2006

LIBRARY AND ARCHIVES CANADA CATALOGUING IN PUBLICATION
Gentlemen, this is a football : football's best quotes & quips / compiled by Eric Zweig.
Includes index.
ISBN-13: 978-1-55407-228-6
ISBN-10: 1-55407-228-X
1. Football—Quotations, maxims, etc. 2. National Football League—Quotations,
maxims, etc. I. Zweig, Eric, 1963-
GV950.5.G45 2006 796.332 C2006-902470-7

Published in the United States by
Firefly Books (U.S.) Inc.
P.O. Box 1338, Ellicott Station
Buffalo, New York 14205

Published in Canada by
Firefly Books Ltd.
66 Leek Crescent
Richmond Hill, Ontario L4B 1H1

Cover and interior design by Sari Naworynski

Printed in Canada

The publisher gratefully acknowledges the financial support for our publishing program by the Government of Canada through the Book Publishing Industry Development Program.

For David, Rob, Steve and Guy, my friends when football meant the most.
And to Jody, Mark and Raymond, my quarterbacks from school.

CONTENTS

INTRODUCTION

"Well kid, signing casts isn't exactly my bag..."
   Joe Theismann, hobbling on crutches with a broken
   ankle, to an eight-year-old boy who had asked for an
   autograph on his own broken wrist

If you saw the play (and anyone who saw it has never forgotten), I know what you're thinking. How could anyone
in his right mind ask Joe Theismann to sign his cast?
Theismann had suffered what is quite possibly the worst
sports injury ever seen on television. An injury so bad, it's
been spoofed on *The Simpsons*!

   Well, I was that eight-year-old boy. In my defense, I did
not ask Theismann for his autograph after the famous
career-ending injury of November 18, 1985. This was after
the significantly less famous, Toronto Argonauts' season-
altering injury suffered on August 3, 1972. Though I work
in hockey now and am known to my friends as a baseball
fan, football was my first love, and Joe Theismann was

my hero. (He did sign my cast, by the way, and I kept it for nearly 20 years, until it had all but disintegrated. Joe probably didn't keep either of his.)

"People break legs all the time in football," Hall of Fame lineman and former *Monday Night Football* analyst Dan Dierdorf told a *Washington Post* columnist on the 20th anniversary of Theismann's injury. "It involves the cracking of a bone, but most times, you can't see it. That night, what you saw was so graphic, and when you watch something that's so far out of the normal, you just gag, but you almost can't help watching it again and again."

Let's face it. Violence is a big part of football. If baseball is a pastime, then football speaks to our technological – and sometimes dangerous – modern lives. In the words of comedian George Carlin, "The object in football is for the quarterback to be on target with his aerial assault, riddling the defense by hitting his receivers with deadly accuracy in spite of the blitz, even if he has to use a shotgun. With short bullet passes and long bombs, he marches his troops into enemy territory, balancing this aerial assault with a sustained ground attack that punches holes in the forward wall of the enemy's defensive line." Football has changed the way we speak, adding words and rewriting definitions in all of our personal dictionaries.

When I did a similar book about baseball last year, it was not surprising to find funny and insightful quotes on a wide range of topics. Football people can be just as funny, and equally insightful, though an awful lot of their most entertaining quotes involve pain – how to handle it and how to inflict it!

It also becomes obvious that people take their football seriously, and that they have for a very long time. John Heisman (for whom the Heisman Trophy was named), played college football in the 1880s and '90s, then coached until 1926 – most notably at Georgia Tech, which beat Tennessee's Cumberland University 222–0 in 1916. Heisman certainly took the game seriously, as the following pep talk illustrates: "Gentlemen, it is better to have died as a small boy than to fumble this football."

But just because football is serious business doesn't mean it's not a lot of fun! I hope you'll have as much fun reading this book as I had putting it together. After all, as Bill Cowher, coach of the Pittsburgh Steelers, said shortly before his team beat the Seattle Seahawks in Super Bowl XL, "Sometimes you love a play. Sometimes you don't like a play. It's an emotional game and I love it. It's three hours of fun."

So enjoy!

"**Ability** is what you're capable of doing. **Motivation** determines what you do. **Attitude** determines how well you do it."

COLLEGE FOOTBALL COACH LOU HOLTZ

"I demand just one thing from Clemson players, and
that is attitude. I want them to think as positively
as the 85-year-old man who married a 25-year-old
woman and ordered a five-bedroom house near an
elementary school."

CLEMSON COACH CHARLIE PELL

"There is a big difference in wanting to and willing to."

UNIVERSITY OF ALABAMA FOOTBALL COACH
PAUL (BEAR) BRYANT

"Good fellows are a dime a dozen, but an aggressive
leader is priceless."

ARMY FOOTBALL COACH RED BLAIK

"Football isn't necessarily won by the best players.
It's won by the team with the best attitude."

WASHINGTON REDSKINS COACH GEORGE ALLEN

"There's a very fine line between winning and
losing. Every team in the NFL has talent, but
attitude is the biggest thing that counts – that,
and playing together as a team. If you can capture
that feeling, then you'll have success."

BUFFALO BILLS LINEBACKER RAY BENTLEY

"One player was lost because he broke his nose. How do you go about getting a nose in condition for football?"

UNIVERSITY OF TEXAS FOOTBALL COACH DARRELL ROYAL, WHEN ASKED IF THE ABNORMAL NUMBER OF LONGHORNS' INJURIES IN 1966 HAD RESULTED FROM POOR PHYSICAL CONDITIONING

"The only thing soft about Larry Csonka is his nose."

AUTHOR AL LEVINE, ON THE MIAMI DOLPHINS FULLBACK WHO HAD BROKEN HIS NOSE ABOUT A DOZEN TIMES

"It was like we were jinxed right from the get-go by the football gods."

TORONTO ARGONAUTS DEFENSIVE BACK DICK THORNTON, ON THE TEAM'S 1972 CAMPAIGN IN WHICH FOUR KEY PLAYERS WERE LOST TO INJURIES BY THE END OF THE FIRST REGULAR-SEASON GAME

"I'm going to send the injured reserve players out for the toss next time."

BALTIMORE COLTS COACH MIKE McCORMACK, AFTER THE TEAM'S CO-CAPTAIN, OFFENSIVE GUARD ROBERT PRATT, PULLED A HAMSTRING RUNNING ONTO THE FIELD FOR THE COIN TOSS

"I wasn't much good. When I went into the line on a fake, I would holler, 'I don't have it.'"

COMEDIAN BOB NEWHART, ON HIS HIGH SCHOOL
FOOTBALL CAREER

"It was a time mix-up. We started playing at nine o'clock and the kickoff was at eight."

HOUSTON OILERS COACH BUM PHILLIPS, ON A
PARTICULARLY BAD GAME

"We were tipping off our plays. Whenever we broke from the huddle, three backs were laughing and one was pale as a ghost."

FORMER HOUSTON OILERS GENERAL MANAGER
JOHN BREEN

"Detroit's so bad this year they might lose their bye week."

COMEDIAN AND MONDAY NIGHT FOOTBALL ANALYST
DENNIS MILLER

"The way the Chargers played, the drug must have been formaldehyde."

CBS ANNOUNCER BILL KURTIS, ON ALLEGATIONS OF DRUG
ABUSE BY THE 1974 SAN DIEGO CHARGERS

"They overwhelmed one, underwhelmed ten and whelmed one."

SPORTSWRITER RED SMITH, ON THE 1-10-1 GREEN BAY
PACKERS

"They should put a sign on the 10-yard line saying THE BUCS STOP HERE."

BROADCASTER JACK HARRIS, ON TAMPA BAY'S WEAK
OFFENSE IN THE BUCCANEERS' EARLY YEARS

"Our biggest mistake was not taking Wake Forest lightly enough."

UNIVERSITY OF OKLAHOMA ASSISTANT COACH
LARRY LACEWELL AFTER THE SOONERS BEAT WAKE
FOREST BY MORE THAN FIFTY POINTS

"It wasn't as easy as you think. It's hard to stay awake that long."

WHITWORTH COLLEGE COACH HUGH CAMPBELL,
ON A 70-30 VICTORY

"The game was not as close as the score indicates."

MICHIGAN STATE FOOTBALL COACH DUFFY DAUGHERTY,
CHASTISING HIS TEAM AFTER A 49-14 LOSS

"It would have been 73 to 7."

WASHINGTON REDSKINS QUARTERBACK SAMMY BAUGH,
WHEN ASKED IF THE OUTCOME MIGHT HAVE BEEN
DIFFERENT IF A TEAMMATE HADN'T DROPPED A POSSIBLE
TOUCHDOWN PASS EARLY IN THE CHICAGO BEARS' 73-0
WIN IN THE 1940 NFL CHAMPIONSHIP GAME

"No wonder you guys got kicked around. Every guy on the team has still got all his teeth."

LOS ANGELES RAMS COACH JOE STYDAHAR, AFTER A
56-20 LOSS TO THE EAGLES IN 1950

"It got to the point where, being a Christian and being a person who loves people, I actually felt sorry for the Broncos."

SAN FRANCISCO 49ERS TACKLE BUBBA PARIS, ON SAN FRANCISCO'S 55–10 ROUT OF DENVER IN SUPER BOWL XXIV

"I'm glad we're not going to the Gator Bowl."

UNIVERSITY OF ARKANSAS COACH **LOU HOLTZ**, ON BEING
PELTED WITH ORANGES BY FANS CELEBRATING THE TEAM'S
INVITATION TO THE ORANGE BOWL

"I've been to the Fiesta Bowl for the past two years. It will certainly be nice to take the team with me."

BRIGHAM YOUNG UNIVERSITY COACH **LAVELL EDWARDS**

"Every year we keep going to a minor bowl. If they
have a Soybean Bowl next year, we'll probably be
in that."

LOUISIANA STATE UNIVERSITY BOARD OF SUPERVISORS
MEMBER **JAKE STAPLES**, ON LSU'S BACK-TO-BACK
APPEARANCES IN THE SUN AND BLUEBONNET BOWLS

"He said: 'Gosh, Dad, that means we're not going to
any more bowl games.'"

FORMER ARIZONA STATE AND OHIO STATE ASSISTANT
JIM COLLETTO, ON HIS 11-YEAR-OLD SON'S REACTION TO
HIS TAKING THE HEAD COACHING JOB AT PURDUE

"He was a star end, a star tackle and a crushing full-back who could pass. I believe 11 Nagurskis could beat 11 Granges or 11 Thorpes."

LEGENDARY SPORTSWRITER GRANTLAND RICE, COMPARING THE IMMORTAL BRONKO NAGURSKI OF THE CHICAGO BEARS TO FELLOW LEGENDS RED GRANGE AND JIM THORPE

"A lot of men have passed in front of me but none with a build like that man."

CHICAGO BEARS LONGTIME OWNER AND COACH GEORGE HALAS, ON BRONKO NAGURSKI

"Running into him was like running into an electric shock."

FOOTBALL LEGEND RED GRANGE, ON FELLOW IMMORTAL BRONKO NAGURSKI

"I think there is less enjoyment now. The quarterback always handles the ball. The game always seems the same. Only the names and numbers change – and the platoons. Remember, we only played with 18 men."

CHICAGO BEARS LEGEND BRONKO NAGURSKI, COMPARING THE NFL OF THE 1930s WITH THE GAME OF THE 1970s

He was the only man I ever saw who
ran his own interference.

NEW YORK GIANTS COACH **STEVE OWEN**, ON BRONKO NAGURSKI

"I'd like to be remembered like that, somebody who stands for hard work and total effort. I want to do everything perfectly on the field – pass blocking, running a dummy route, carrying out a fake, all of it."

CHICAGO BEARS RUNNING BACK WALTER PAYTON

"Each and every day, Jerome is always teaching me something about what it takes to be a professional athlete. The way he's handled his whole career, each and every year he's bringing his lunch pail to work. I'm very blessed to have him in my career."

PITTSBURGH STEELERS RECEIVER HINES WARD,
ON TEAMMATE JEROME BETTIS

"The one I'm most proud of is the interception record because that one built the most character and that's the one that gives you that tough back-bone."

FORMER LOUISIANA TECH QUARTERBACK AND CFL STAR
MATT DUNIGAN, ON BREAKING SO MANY OF TERRY
BRADSHAW'S SCHOOL RECORDS

"When he played, he left his heart on the field. And unfortunately for Michael he played that way on the football field, and he played that way off the football field. You can't turn it off sometimes."

FORMER DALLAS COWBOYS RUNNING BACK EMMITT SMITH, ON TEAMMATE MICHAEL IRVIN, WHOSE OFF-FIELD INDIS-CRETIONS MAY BE HURTING HIS HALL OF FAME CHANCES

"There are three types of football players.
First, there are those who are winners and know they are winners.
Then there are the losers who know they're losers.
Then there are those who aren't winners but don't know it.
They're the ones for me.
They never quit trying.
They're the soul of our game."

UNIVERSITY OF ALABAMA FOOTBALL COACH PAUL (BEAR) BRYANT

"I'm trying to be a good teammate here... Let's just say we had some problems in protection."

INDIANAPOLIS COLTS QUARTERBACK **PEYTON MANNING**, BLAMING THE OFFENSIVE LINE FOR THE TEAM'S POOR SHOWING IN ITS 21-18 LOSS TO PITTSBURGH IN THE 2006 PLAYOFFS

"That's a good assessment, I would agree with that, just with what he brings to the table. A number of commentators will say he's a warrior, he's played with injuries. I feel like him being knowledgeable about the quarterback position, I feel like we'd probably be in a better situation."

PHILADELPHIA EAGLES RECEIVER TERRELL OWENS, AGREEING WITH INTERVIEWER MICHAEL IRVIN THAT THE TEAM WOULD BE BETTER OFF WITH GREEN BAY'S BRETT FAVRE AT QUARTERBACK

"It was definitely a slap in the face to me. It was a slap in the face because, as deep as people want to go into it, it was black-on-black crime."

PHILADELPHIA EAGLES QUARTERBACK DONOVAN McNABB, RESPONDING TO TERRELL OWENS' CRITICISM

"I'm not the one who got tired in the Super Bowl."

PHILADELPHIA EAGLES RECEIVER TERRELL OWENS, TAKING ANOTHER SHOT AT DONOVAN McNABB

"I'm not a real big Colts fan right now, unfortunately. I just don't see us getting better. All week
before the Jets game I'm like, '[No.] 18, we're going
to handle it, me and you we're going to win this
game.' And he's like, 'Yeah, yeah, OK.' And I'm like,
'Peyton, show some enthusiasm, you're the quarterback and we need to win this game.' I just don't see
it from him."

INDIANAPOLIS COLTS KICKER MIKE VANDERJAGT,
CRITICIZING QUARTERBACK PEYTON MANNING AFTER
A 41-0 PLAYOFF LOSS TO THE NEW YORK JETS

"Here we are, I'm out at my third Pro Bowl, I'm
about to go in and throw a touchdown to Jerry
Rice, we're honoring the Hall of Fame, and we're
talking about our idiot kicker who got liquored up
and ran his mouth off. The sad thing is, he's a good
kicker. He's a good kicker. But he's an idiot."

INDIANAPOLIS COLTS QUARTERBACK PEYTON MANNING,
RESPONDING TO THE CRITICISM

"If God wanted women to understand men, football would never have been created."

WRITER ROGER SIMON

"It's sort of like a beauty contest. It's very easy to pick the top one, two or three girls, but then the rest of them look the same. It's like that in scouting."

PRO FOOTBALL SCOUT GIL BRANDT

"He's like a beautiful woman who can't cook, doesn't want to clean and doesn't want to take care of the kids. You really don't want her, but she's so beautiful that you can't let her go."

PLAYER TURNED TV COMMENTATOR DEION SANDERS, COMMENTING ON PROBLEM RECEIVER RANDY MOSS

"Tom Landry is a perfectionist. If he was married to Raquel Welch, he'd expect her to cook."

DALLAS COWBOYS QUARTERBACK DON MEREDITH, ON HIS COACH

"Never get married in the morning, cause you never know who you'll meet that night."

GREEN BAY PACKERS GREAT PAUL HORNUNG

"I don't know. I haven't seen the films yet."

SAN DIEGO CHARGERS ASSISTANT COACH FORREST GREGG, WHEN ASKED HOW HIS HONEYMOON WAS

"Probably the best draft pick I've ever made."

NEW YORK JETS COACH ERIC MANGINI, THANKING HIS WIFE FOR HER SUPPORT

"Boats. Planes. Cars. Clothes. Blondes. Brunettes. Redheads. All so pretty. I love them all."

NEW YORK JETS PLAYBOY QUARTERBACK JOE NAMATH

"Who wants to go with a guy who's got two bad knees and a quick release?"

ACTRESS CONNIE STEVENS, ON JOE NAMATH

"I recruited a Czech kicker, and during the eye examination, the doctor asked him if he could read the bottom line. 'Read it!' the Czech kicker said, 'I know him.'"

OHIO STATE FOOTBALL COACH **WOODY HAYES**

"I'm a firm believer that all sports will eventually be global. Someday, we may have a quarterback from China named Yao Fling."

NFL COMMISSIONER **PAUL TAGLIABUE**

"He's gonna be a real good kicker this year if he can get by foreign language. English is his foreign language."

FLORIDA STATE COACH **LARRY JONES**, ON CYPRUS-BORN KICKER AHMET ASKIN

"You battle for 59 minutes, and then some little guy with a clean uniform comes in to kick a field goal to win the game, and he says, 'Hooray, I keek a touchdown.'"

DETROIT LIONS DEFENSIVE TACKLE **ALEX KARRAS**, DERIDING KICKERS LIKE HIS TEAMMATE GARO YEPREMIAN OF CYPRUS, WHO LATER USED THIS AS THE TITLE OF HIS AUTOBIOGRAPHY

"They ought to tighten the immigration laws."

MINNESOTA VIKINGS COACH **NORM VAN BROCKLIN**, AFTER DETROIT'S GARO YEPREMIAN KICKED SIX FIELD GOALS TO BEAT HIS TEAM

"I don't hire anybody not brighter than I am. If they're not brighter than I am, I don't need them."

UNIVERSITY OF ALABAMA FOOTBALL COACH
PAUL (BEAR) BRYANT

"A good coach needs a patient wife, a loyal dog, and a great quarterback, but not necessarily in that order."

MINNESOTA VIKINGS COACH BUD GRANT

"If they want to use artificial turf, let them find artificial players."

MIAMI DOLPHINS LINEBACKER DOUG SWIFT

"Mug him on the way out of the locker room."

NEW YORK GIANTS LINEBACKER SAM HUFF, ON HOW TO
STOP LEGENDARY CLEVELAND BROWNS RUNNING BACK
JIM BROWN

"You could give your outside linebackers hand grenades."

CLEVELAND BROWNS COACH SAM RUTIGLIANO, WHEN
ASKED HOW TO STOP SEATTLE QUARTERBACK JIM ZORN
FROM SCRAMBLING

"When you win, say nothing. When you lose, say less."

CLEVELAND BROWNS COACH PAUL BROWN

"We're going to win Sunday. I'll guarantee you."

NEW YORK JETS QUARTERBACK **JOE NAMATH,** ON THE THURSDAY BEFORE SUPER BOWL III AGAINST THE 21-POINT FAVORITE BALTIMORE COLTS

"Guaranteed it, huh? Well, I'm with him. Joe's an honest boy. I don't think he's whistling Dixie."

NEW YORK JETS COACH **WEEB EWBANK,** WHEN TOLD ABOUT NAMATH'S GUARANTEE

"Joe's talking down here may be worth two touchdowns to the Colts. They were going into the game
red hot. Now they're white hot."

FORMER COLTS RUNNING BACK BUDDY YOUNG

"Hasn't that Namath learned yet to keep quiet?
Doesn't he know if he keeps his mouth shut he
won't lose his teeth?"

BALTIMORE COLTS DEFENSIVE TACKLE BILLY RAY SMITH

"I felt loose, real loose. My arm was so loose I
thought it was going to fall off."

NEW YORK JETS QUARTERBACK JOE NAMATH, DENYING
HE FELT ANY EXTRA PRESSURE IN SUPER BOWL III

"You know me. That is the way I talk. I felt we'd
win, but I wasn't trying to be cocky."

NEW YORK JETS QUARTERBACK JOE NAMATH, AFTER
BEATING THE COLTS IN SUPER BOWL III

"I had a Cadillac offered to me a couple of times. You know how that works? They give you the Cadillac one year, and the next they give you the gas to get out of town."

OHIO STATE FOOTBALL COACH WOODY HAYES

"We're in a performance-now business, and I don't think you take anything for granted. I'm not so naïve to think that if we have a bad year, I won't be another one of those guys that shows up on Black Monday."

LONGTIME PITTSBURGH STEELERS COACH BILL COWHER

"I'm on a one-year renewal, and I'm not trusting my paycheck to someone on a four-year scholarship."

UNIVERSITY OF IOWA COACH BOB CUMMINGS, ON WHY HE CALLED THE PLAYS

"We're building a house on Long Island. That's pretty optimistic – a little like doing a crossword puzzle with a pen."

NEW YORK JETS COACH LOU HOLTZ, COMMENTING ON JOB SECURITY WHEN HE WAS HIRED IN 1976. (HE QUIT AFTER THE TEAM WON JUST THREE OF ITS FIRST THIRTEEN GAMES.)

"I left because of illness and fatigue. The fans were sick and tired of me."

FORMER DENVER BRONCOS COACH JOHN RALSTON

"You can have three great seasons and then lose, and it's 'What have you done for me lately?'"

BIG EAST COMMISSIONER MIKE TRANGHESE, EXPLAINING WHY HE THINKS THERE'LL BE NO MORE COACHES WITH THE LONGEVITY OF PENN STATE'S JOE PATERNO

"Every coach is in the last year of his contract. Some just don't know it."

CAROLINA PANTHERS OFFENSIVE COORDINATOR (AND FORMER FALCONS AND CHARGERS HEAD COACH) DAN HENNING

"If you're a coach, NFL stands for 'Not For Long.'"

NFL COACH TURNED TV COMMENTATOR JERRY GLANVILLE

"Changing coaches, all that does is make you an expansion team."

PITTSBURGH STEELERS CHAIRMAN DAN ROONEY. THE STEELERS HAVE ONLY HAD TWO COACHES SINCE 1969

"We know these people; these people know us...
We have a connection to these people."

COLTS QUARTERBACK **PEYTON MANNING**, ON THE FANS IN
INDIANAPOLIS

"Here, being a football player is like being a
Hollywood celebrity in Hollywood. You could walk
next to Brad Pitt and the fans would say, 'Oh, wow,
that guy is on the practice squad for the Steelers.'
They wouldn't even notice Brad Pitt. That's the
great thing about Pittsburgh and how fanatic they
are about it."

PITTSBURGH STEELERS SAFETY **TROY POLAMALU**

This is the best place for guys to come and focus on nothing but football.

PACKERS QUARTERBACK **BRETT FAVRE** ON PLAYING IN
GREEN BAY

"The street to obscurity is paved with athletes who perform great feats before friendly crowds. Greatness in major league sports is the ability to win in a stadium filled with people who are pulling for you to lose."

WASHINGTON REDSKINS COACH GEORGE ALLEN

"When you come to Pittsburgh you are playing forty players and 50,000 fans."

PITTSBURGH STEELERS RUNNING BACK FRENCHY FUQUA

"Sure, the home field is an advantage – but so is having a lot of talent."

MIAMI DOLPHINS QUARTERBACK DAN MARINO

"We're so far away from most of the country, only Lewis and Clark know where we are."

SEATTLE SEAHAWKS VICE PRESIDENT GARY WRIGHT, ON HIS TEAM'S LACK OF MEDIA ATTENTION

"There's no system of play that substitutes for knocking an opponent down. When you hit, hit hard."

FOOTBALL COACH POP WARNER

"Football is not a contact sport. Football is a collision sport. Dancing is a contact sport."

MICHIGAN STATE FOOTBALL COACH DUFFY DAUGHERTY

"I had a license to kill for 60 minutes a week. It was like going totally insane."

DETROIT LIONS DEFENSIVE LINEMAN ALEX KARRAS

"I wouldn't ever set out to hurt anyone deliberately unless it was, you know, important – like a league game or something."

CHICAGO BEARS LINEBACKER DICK BUTKUS

"Dick rattles your brains when he tackles you."

GREEN BAY PACKERS QUARTERBACK BART STARR,
ON CHICAGO BEARS LINEBACKER DICK BUTKUS

"I like to believe that my **best hits** border on **felonious assault.**"

OAKLAND RAIDERS DEFENSIVE BACK **JACK TATUM,** WHO WAS KNOWN AS "THE ASSASSIN"

"People get hurt all the time in football. It's part of what we do."

NEW YORK GIANTS LINEBACKER LAWRENCE TAYLOR

"We try to hurt everybody. We hit each other as hard as we can. This is a man's game."

NEW YORK GIANTS LINEBACKER SAM HUFF

"We used to call Doug Plank "Bullet" because he just loved to hit people."

CHICAGO BEARS LINEBACKER DOUG BUFFONE, ON THE TEAM'S STRONG SAFETY

"I'm an artist. Only my art is to assault people."

OAKLAND/LOS ANGELES RAIDERS DEFENSIVE END HOWIE LONG

"He knocked me woozy. I have never been hit like that before and, hopefully, I'll never be hit like that again."

NOTRE DAME QUARTERBACK STEVE BEUERLEIN, AFTER BEING TACKLED BY ALABAMA'S CORNELIUS BENNETT

"It is better to give a lick than receive one. If any-body got in my way, I tried to run right through them."

LOS ANGELES RAIDERS RUNNING BACK (AND MULTI-SPORT STAR) BO JACKSON

"He knocks the hell out of people, but in a Christian way."

WASHINGTON REDSKINS QUARTERBACK (AND TEXAS CHRISTIAN UNIVERSITY ALUM) SAMMY BAUGH, ON A VERY RELIGIOUS LINEBACKER

"I guess people think the Bears keep me in a cage and only let me out on Sundays to play football. Nobody thinks I can talk, much less write my own name."

LEGENDARY CHICAGO BEARS LINEBACKER **DICK BUTKUS**, WHO DID NOT APPRECIATE HIS NICKNAME "THE ANIMAL"

"I resent being called a bulldozer or a battering ram. It reflects a certain type of mentality. There's an ability to react to an opening that I have, and not many people have it."

MIAMI DOLPHINS FULLBACK LARRY CSONKA

"It's gotten to the point where I can't say something in jest without being taken seriously."

DALLAS COWBOYS QUARTERBACK ROGER STAUBACH,
ON HIS CLEAN-CUT IMAGE

"The only perfect man who ever lived had a beard and long hair and didn't wear shoes and slept in barns and didn't hold a regular job and never put on a tie. I'm not comparing myself to Him – I'm in enough trouble trying to stack up against Bart Starr – but I'm saying that you don't judge a man by the way he cuts his hair. Shoot, I never saw a picture of a saint who didn't have long hair. Abraham Lincoln had a beard, and George Washington wore a wig."

NEW YORK JETS QUARTERBACK JOE NAMATH,
DEFENDING HIS HAIRSTYLE AGAINST THE CONSERVATIVE
NFL ESTABLISHMENT

"What is a medium collateral whatever ligament? It sounds like spaghetti with fish sauce."

FORMER BALTIMORE COLTS DEFENSIVE LINEMAN
ART DONOVAN

"I don't know what he has. A pulled groin. A hip flexor. I don't know. A pulled something. I never pulled anything. You can't pull fat."

NEW YORK JETS COACH **BRUCE COSLET**

"When you get old, everything is hurting. When I get up in the morning, it sounds like I'm making popcorn."

NEW YORK GIANTS LINEBACKER **LAWRENCE TAYLOR**

"John Riggins, like Joe Namath, is a riddle wrapped in a bandage."

SPORTS COMMENTATOR **LARRY MERCHANT**

"When Nature designed the male knee, she obviously had neither football nor walking shorts in mind."

WRITER **BILL VAUGHAN**

"It may be that your body reaches a point all at once where you are more prone to injury, and it seems to me that I have probably reached that point."

BALTIMORE COLTS RECEIVER **RAYMOND BERRY**, ANNOUNCING HIS RETIREMENT AS A PLAYER

"I've never looked at myself as injury-prone. I've looked at myself as injury-plagued. I've been a part of some very bad luck."

NEW YORK JETS QUARTERBACK **CHAD PENNINGTON**

"Joe has a 22-year-old body and 70-year-old knees."

A NEW YORK JETS **TEAMMATE**, ON JOE NAMATH

"I have a pair of legs that only an orthopedic surgeon could love."

NEW YORK JETS QUARTERBACK **JOE NAMATH**

"My knees look like they lost a knife fight with a midget."

KANSAS CITY CHIEFS LINEBACKER **E.J. HOLUB**, AFTER HIS TWELFTH KNEE OPERATION

"I can't even limp."

UNIVERSITY OF MINNESOTA LINEMAN JEFF MORROW,
ON THE SEVERITY OF INJURIES TO HIS RIGHT KNEE AND
LEFT ANKLE

"The pads don't keep you from getting hurt. They just keep you from getting killed."

INDIANAPOLIS COLTS DEFENSIVE END CHAD BRATZKE

"Ever since they put this pin in I've been getting great reception on my car radio. I wonder what will happen when I try to get on an airplane?"

MIAMI DOLPHIN BOB KUECHENBERG, ON PLAYING WITH A
STEEL PIN IN HIS BROKEN ARM

"It didn't do any good. My neck still hurts."

TAMPA BAY BUCCANEERS GUARD IRA GORDON, AFTER
HAVING HIS INJURED NECK X-RAYED

"He sits home and watches his bones mend."

PATRICIA PHILLIPS, WIFE OF SAN FRANCISCO 49ERS
DEFENSIVE BACK MEL PHILLIPS, ON WHAT HER HUSBAND
DOES IN THE OFF-SEASON

"Physically, he's a world-beater. Mentally, he's an egg-beater."

UNIVERSITY OF MICHIGAN CENTER MATT ELLIOTT, DESCRIBING OHIO STATE LINEBACKER ALONZO SPELLMAN

"If Bud Grant and Tom Landry were in a personality contest, it would be a 0–0 draw."

DALLAS COWBOYS QUARTERBACK TURNED TV COMMENTATOR DON MEREDITH, ON TWO OF THE NFL'S LEAST COLORFUL COACHES

"The scouts said I looked like Tarzan and played like Jane."

PHILADELPHIA EAGLES 6'8", 275-POUND DEFENSIVE END DENNIS HARRISON, ON WHY HE WAS PASSED OVER IN THE FIRST THREE ROUNDS OF THE 1978 NFL DRAFT

"If they don't want 'em to get hit, why don't they just put a dress on 'em?"

PITTSBURGH STEELERS LINEBACKER JACK LAMBERT, ON QUARTERBACKS

"Adams is the most versatile player who ever came to the Bears. So far we've found he can't play six positions."

A CHICAGO BEARS AIDE, ON 1959 DRAFT CHOICE
JOHN ADAMS

"As for you, Benbrook, I don't think you could get out of a greenhouse with an ax."

UNIVERSITY OF MICHIGAN FOOTBALL COACH
FIELDING YOST, UNHAPPY WITH THE FIRST-HALF
PERFORMANCE OF ALL-AMERICAN GUARD AL BENBROOK

"The trouble with Ford is he played too many years without a helmet."

PRESIDENT LYNDON JOHNSON, ON FUTURE PRESIDENT
(AND FORMER COLLEGE FOOTBALL PLAYER) GERALD FORD

"He's a nice guy. But if they had a Naïve Bowl, he'd coach both sides."

SPORTSWRITER ORVILLE HENRY, ON TEXAS CHRISTIAN
UNIVERSITY FOOTBALL COACH JIM SHOFNER

"He can be a great player in this league for a long time if he learns to say two words: 'I'm full.'"

NFL COACH TURNED TV COMMENTATOR JERRY GLANVILLE, ON ROOKIE LINCOLN KENNEDY WHO REPORTED OVER-WEIGHT AT 300 POUNDS

"When we stick him in the whirlpool, we gotta have a lifeguard on duty."

FLORIDA STATE COACH BOBBY BOWDEN, ON A 5'8", 135-POUND FRESHMAN

"A bunch of banjo-playing inbreds."

WINNIPEG BLUE BOMBERS KICKER TROY WESTWOOD, JOKING ABOUT FANS OF THE RIVAL SASKATCHEWAN ROUGHRIDERS

"But the real tragedy was that 15 hadn't been colored yet."

UNIVERSITY OF FLORIDA FOOTBALL COACH STEVE SPURRIER, TELLING GATORS FANS THAT A FIRE AT AUBURN'S FOOTBALL DORM HAD DESTROYED 20 BOOKS

"I'm cool on the outside, but on the inside it's like a thousand little kids jumping up and down on Christmas morning."

MINNESOTA VIKING CHUCK FOREMAN, WHO DID NOT
CELEBRATE HIS TOUCHDOWNS

"I don't like the showmanship. Sometimes it's too much."

FORMER CINCINNATI BENGAL ICKEY WOODS, FAMOUS IN
THE LATE 1980s FOR HIS ICKEY SHUFFLE TOUCHDOWN
DANCE, ON ESCALATING END ZONE ANTICS

"Someday they'll have offsetting 15-yard dance penalties."

NFL COACH TURNED TV COMMENTATOR JERRY GLANVILLE,
AFTER AN EARLY NFL EFFORT TO PROHIBIT CELEBRATIONS
ON THE FIELD

"I'm looking forward to seeing what Chad will come up with to celebrate now."

INDIANAPOLIS COLTS COACH TONY DUNGY, AFTER THE
2006 CRACKDOWN, ON CINCINNATI BENGALS RECEIVER
CHAD JOHNSON, WHOSE TOUCHDOWN CELEBRATIONS
HAD INCLUDED PUTTING THE BALL WITH AN END ZONE
PYLON AND DROPPING TO A KNEE TO PROPOSE TO A
CHEERLEADER

"It's like being in a huddle with God."

BALTIMORE COLTS TIGHT END JOHN MACKEY, ON HALL OF
FAME QUARTERBACK JOHNNY UNITAS

"It's like holding group therapy for 50,000 people a
week."

WASHINGTON REDSKIN SONNY JURGENSEN, ON PLAYING
QUARTERBACK

"He is to passing what Lindbergh was to the airplane."

FOOTBALL HISTORIAN KEVIN ROBERTS, ON WASHINGTON
REDSKINS QUARTERBACK SAMMY BAUGH

"He's like a state fair. He gets bigger and better
every year."

NEW ORLEANS SAINTS QUARTERBACK ARCHIE MANNING
(FATHER OF PEYTON AND ELI), ON LOS ANGELES RAMS
VETERAN DEFENSIVE TACKLE MERLIN OLSEN

"A bowling ball rolling downhill."

DENVER BRONCOS
DEFENSIVE LINEMAN
GERARD WARREN,
DESCRIBING PITTSBURGH
STEELERS RUNNING
BACK JEROME BETTIS

"Playing cornerback is like being on an island; people can see you, but they can't help you."

SAN FRANCISCO 49ERS CORNERBACK EDDIE LEWIS

"Dick Butkus was like Moby Dick in a goldfish bowl."

NFL FILMS PRESIDENT STEVE SABOL

"It was as if a locomotive had hit me and been followed by a ten-ton truck rambling over the remains."

NOTRE DAME FOOTBALL COACH KNUTE ROCKNE, RECALLING WHAT IT HAD BEEN LIKE TO PLAY AGAINST JIM THORPE

"It was like having a redwood tree fall on you."

CHICAGO BEARS OWNER, COACH AND FORMER PLAYER GEORGE HALAS, ON HIS MEMORIES OF BEING TACKLED BY JIM THORPE

"**Tackling Bronko was like trying to stop a freight train going downhill.**"

FOOTBALL LEGEND ERNIE NEVERS, ON BRONKO NAGURSKI

"Ah, you always get a little nervous. Honestly, I don't think that ever really, really goes away. That excitement kind of helps elevate your awareness and kind of gets you focused more."

KICKER **ADAM VINATIERI**, WHO WON TWO SUPER BOWLS FOR THE NEW ENGLAND PATRIOTS WITH LAST-SECOND KICKS

"I'm relied upon to score three points when we need three points with 20 seconds to go. I should have made it."

MIKE VANDERJAGT, THE MOST ACCURATE KICKER IN NFL HISTORY, AFTER MISSING A LAST-SECOND KICK IN THE INDIANAPOLIS COLTS' 2006 PLAYOFF LOSS TO PITTSBURGH. THE COLTS LET HIM GO AFTER THE SEASON AND SIGNED ADAM VINATIERI

"One thing I've learned over the years is sometimes if you make kicks early in the game, you don't have to make them late."

KICKER GARY ANDERSON, THE NFL'S ALL-TIME SCORING LEADER

"Maybe it's a kick that puts you through, but you have to approach it the same. You don't vary anything."

PITTSBURGH STEELERS KICKER JEFF REED, WHO WAS A PERFECT FIVE-FOR-FIVE IN HIS CAREER IN GAME-WINNING FIELD GOALS HEADING INTO SUPER BOWL XL

"I'd rather win 55–0 if you want to know the truth."

SEATTLE SEAHAWKS KICKER JOSH BROWN, ON HIS FEELINGS ABOUT A CHANCE TO KICK THE GAME-WINNING FIELD GOAL IN SUPER BOWL XL

"He plays middle linebacker like a piranha."

SCOUT AND FUTURE NEW YORK JETS COACH JOE WALTON,
ON DICK BUTKUS OF THE CHICAGO BEARS

"Other guys like Baltimore's Mike Curtis and
Chicago's Dick Butkus thrive on that man-eating
image. I never have cared for it."

MIAMI DOLPHINS LINEBACKER NICK BUONICONTI, WHO
ENJOYED A HALL OF FAME CAREER WHILE WORKING AS A
LAWYER IN THE OFF-SEASON

"If they did, I'd stomp 'em and do a pirouette on
their heads."

CINCINNATI BENGALS LINEBACKER KEN AVERY, WHEN
ASKED IF ANYONE EVER CALLED HIM A SISSY BECAUSE HE
STUDIED BALLET

**" I'm the one
you need to be worried about."**

TATTOO ON THE LEFT BICEPS OF PITTSBURGH STEELERS
LINEBACKER LARRY FOOTE

"Playing middle linebacker is like walking through a
lion's cage in a three-piece porkchop suit."

TAMPA BAY BUCCANEERS LINEBACKER CECIL JOHNSON

If you aren't fired with enthusiasm, you'll be fired with enthusiasm."

VINCE LOMBARDI

"Gentlemen, this is a football."

GREEN BAY PACKERS COACH VINCE LOMBARDI, HOLDING
UP A BALL IN FRONT OF HIS PLAYERS AND LETTING THEM
KNOW IT WAS TIME TO GET BACK TO BASICS

"There is Eastern Standard Time and Greenwich
Time and then there is Lombardi Time – fifteen
minutes early. If you come ten minutes early,
they've started without you."

GREEN BAY PACKERS KICKER DON CHANDLER

"There's a second-place bowl game, and it's a hinky-
dink football game, held in a hinky-dink town,
played by hinky-dink football players. That's all
second place is: hinky-dink."

VINCE LOMBARDI

"The spirit, the will to win, and the will to excel are
the things that endure. These qualities are so much
more important than the events that occur."

VINCE LOMBARDI

"Lombardi treats us all the same – like dogs."

GREEN BAY PACKERS DEFENSIVE TACKLE HENRY JORDAN

"When he says sit down, I don't even bother to look for a chair."

GREEN BAY PACKERS TIGHT END **MAX McGEE**,
ON VINCE LOMBARDI

"He united us, initially, in our fear of him, our hatred for him. He was, deliberately, the common enemy, the focus of all our frustrations. If our muscles ached, it was Lombardi's fault. If our nerves were frayed, it was Lombardi's fault. If our mind reeled, it was Lombardi's fault. The fierceness of Lombardi, combined with the smallness of the city in which we played, forced upon us camaraderie and a close-ness that, nurtured by victory, grew into love."

GREEN BAY PACKERS GUARD AND AUTHOR **JERRY KRAMER**

"One night, after a long, cold difficult day, Lombardi came home late and tumbled into bed. 'God,' said his wife, 'your feet are cold.' And Lombardi answered, 'Around the house, dear, you may call me Vince.'"

GREEN BAY PACKERS HALFBACK **PAUL HORNUNG**,
ON VINCE LOMBARDI

"Sure, luck means a lot in football. Not having a good quarterback is bad luck."

MIAMI DOLPHINS COACH **DON SHULA**

"By nature, I'm aggressive. I'll take shots, I'll take chances; therefore, you have mistakes."

GREEN BAY PACKERS QUARTERBACK **BRETT FAVRE**, ON WHY HE THROWS SO MANY INTERCEPTIONS

"OK, it's a risk. But hey, I'm a poker player. You can take it to the river. I'm not scared to make a change. I'm not scared to go out on a limb and try something different."

FORMER INDIANAPOLIS COLTS RUNNING BACK **EDGERRIN JAMES**, ON HIS DECISION TO SIGN WITH THE ARIZONA CARDINALS

"Maybe the difference in football is your mistakes come in front of several million people. Most people's mistakes are buried someplace."

WASHINGTON REDSKINS COACH **JOE GIBBS**

"**You have a chance to make a big play, you take it. Because you don't know when you'll get your next opportunity. It's not like I'm thinking, waiting, 'Well, should I do it, shouldn't I do it?' You just react.**"

FORMER MIAMI DOLPHINS QUARTERBACK DAN MARINO, ATTRIBUTING HIS SUCCESS TO AN ABSENCE OF FEAR

"Some coaches pray for wisdom. I pray for 260-pound tackles. They'll give me plenty of wisdom."

WAKE FOREST UNIVERSITY COACH CHUCK MILLS

"Football is more mental than physical, no matter how it looks from the stands."

GREEN BAY PACKERS LINEBACKER RAY NITSCHKE

"Most football players are temperamental. That's 90 percent temper and 10 percent mental."

FORMER CHICAGO BEARS SAFETY DOUG PLANK

"Playing in the NFL is 10 percent mental, 90 percent Hollywood."

PHILADELPHIA EAGLES RECEIVER TERRELL OWENS

"If I was a goody-goody, I'd be a psychological wreck."

LEGENDARY CLEVELAND BROWNS RUNNING BACK
JIM BROWN, ON HIS LIFE OFF THE FOOTBALL FIELD

"Everybody is not going to be squeaky clean."

TROUBLEMAKING RECEIVER TERRELL OWENS

"I don't think I've been asked this many questions since my mother caught me drinking in high school."

MIAMI DOLPHINS THIRD-STRING QUARTERBACK
DON STROCK, FACING THE MEDIA AFTER HIS FIRST START

"You have to play this game like somebody just hit your mother with a two-by-four."

OAKLAND RAIDERS DEFENSIVE LINEMAN DAN BIRDWELL

"If my mother put on a helmet and shoulder pads and a uniform that wasn't the same as the one I was wearing, I'd run over her if she was in my way. And I love my mother."

LOS ANGELES RAIDERS RUNNING BACK (AND MULTI-SPORT STAR) BO JACKSON

"I'd run over my own mother to win the Super Bowl."

WASHINGTON REDSKINS LINEMAN JOE JACOBY, BEFORE SUPER BOWL XVIII VERSUS THE RAIDERS

"To win, I'd run over Joe's mom, too."

LOS ANGELES RAIDERS LINEBACKER MATT MILLEN

"No player is worth a million dollars.
I can understand why a player would
have an agent. I couldn't keep from
laughing if I went in and demanded a
million from an owner."

CHICAGO BEARS LEGEND RED GRANGE

"I gave George Allen an unlimited budget and he exceeded it.

WASHINGTON REDSKINS OWNER EDWARD BENNETT WILLIAMS, ON WHY HE FIRED HIS HEAD COACH

"Even though I had a good year, my salary was cut to $4,500 my second year and the year after that to $3,700 where it stayed for a number of years. When I asked for $6,000 in 1938 [after making $5,000 in 1937], they turned me down. I went home figuring they'd call me, but they never did. Not until five years later."

CHICAGO BEARS LEGEND BRONKO NAGURSKI, ON THE NFL DURING THE DEPRESSION AND WORLD WAR II

"A lot of players didn't have agents then. We couldn't understand why we should pay an agent a commission for not getting us the same salary we couldn't get on our own."

PITTSBURGH STEELERS QUARTERBACK TURNED COMMENTATOR TERRY BRADSHAW, ON CONTRACT NEGOTIATIONS IN THE EARLY 1970s

"Agents today make more money for negotiating rookie contracts than I made for playing."

PITTSBURGH STEELERS QUARTERBACK TURNED COMMENTATOR TERRY BRADSHAW

"The irony is that the sport with the most devastating rate of injury has the least guarantees."

AGENT LEIGH STEINBERG, ON THE LACK OF GUARANTEED CONTRACTS IN THE NFL

"What concerned people is if you guaranteed someone satisfaction in this highly competitive sport, would he compete the way he would if the money were not guaranteed?"

FORMER DALLAS COWBOYS VICE PRESIDENT OF PLAYER PERSONNEL GIL BRANDT, ON THE LACK OF GUARANTEED CONTRACTS IN THE NFL

"Players love signing bonuses. They love the big payday and consider it the only time they'll ever have one. Now, it's kind of expected."

NFL PLAYERS ASSOCIATION LAWYER RICHARD BERTHELSEN, ON THE ONLY GUARANTEED MONEY IN AN NFL PLAYERS' CONTRACT

"If he doesn't sign, we lose him. If he does sign, I go broke."

ATLANTA FALCONS OWNER RANKIN SMITH, ON THE TROUBLE SIGNING DRAFT CHOICES DURING THE DAYS OF THE WORLD FOOTBALL LEAGUE

"I got a million-dollar offer from the WFL — one dollar a year for a million years."

JOURNEYMAN OFFENSIVE TACKLE STEVE WRIGHT, ON A BIG-MONEY OFFER FROM THE RIVAL WORLD FOOTBALL LEAGUE

"In 1931, I signed with Portsmouth for $140 a game. That was good money. A lot of players made $95 or $100."

HALL OF FAMER EARL (DUTCH) CLARK, WHO LED THE NFL IN SCORING THREE TIMES IN SEVEN SEASONS WITH PORTSMOUTH AND DETROIT IN THE 1930s

"I never thought my biggest worry would be income taxes."

DALLAS COWBOYS DEFENSIVE TACKLE BOB LILLY

"Players are different today. They don't understand that it's a privilege to play this game. It's an honor. You have an opportunity to make a lot of money. But when you're complaining about only making $7 million to feed your family, nobody has sympathy for that. You're going to turn people off."

FORMER DALLAS COWBOYS RUNNING BACK TONY DORSETT

"It's basically receiver money. David wants to be a receiver in this league and feels he should be paid receiver money."

AGENT MARK CLOUSER, ON THE NEW FIVE-YEAR CONTRACT FOR NEW YORK GIANT DAVID TYREE THAT MADE HIM THE NFL'S HIGHEST-PAID SPECIAL TEAMS PLAYER

"What I find sometimes is that all of us may have too much money. Players. Owners. TV. It's like pigs fighting in a trough, and sometimes we don't appreciate what we have."

NFL EXECUTIVE MIKE BROWN

❝Anybody who says they aren't in it for the money is full of sh...❞

OAKLAND RAIDERS RECEIVER FRED BILETNIKOFF

"Nobody in football should be called a genius. A genius is a guy like Norman Einstein."

WASHINGTON REDSKINS QUARTERBACK TURNED COMMENTATOR JOE THEISMANN, WHO HAD A CHILDHOOD FRIEND NAMED NORMAN EINSTEIN

"Mark Gastineau has got an IQ of about room temperature."

CHICAGO BEARS DEFENSIVE LINEMAN DAN HAMPTON, ON HIS NEW YORK JETS RIVAL

" Every time you make a football player think, you're handicappin' him. "

HOUSTON OILERS COACH BUM PHILLIPS

"The only qualifications for a lineman are to be big and dumb. To be a back you only have to be dumb."

NOTRE DAME FOOTBALL COACH KNUTE ROCKNE

"I took all the tests and realized the guy knocked some sense into me. I'm actually smarter than I was before."

SEATTLE SEAHAWKS RUNNING BACK SHAUN ALEXANDER, CLEARED TO PLAY AFTER SUFFERING A CONCUSSION THE WEEK BEFORE

"Let's face it. The reason you're playing offense is because you ain't good enough to play defense. When you play guard, it's because you aren't smart enough to be a quarterback, not fast enough to be a halfback, not rugged enough to be a fullback, not big enough to be a tackle, and you don't have the hands of an end."

UNIVERSITY OF GEORGIA OFFENSIVE LINE COACH
DICK BESTWICK

"He's big as a gorilla and strong as a gorilla. Now, if he was smart as a gorilla, he'd be fine."

UNIVERSITY OF ALABAMA ASSISTANT COACH SAM BAILEY,
ON A FRESHMAN PLAYER

"In Montana, they renamed a town after an all-time great, Joe Montana. Well, a town in Massachusetts changed their name to honor my guy Terry Bradshaw – Marblehead."

PLAYER TURNED TV COMMENTATOR HOWIE LONG,
JOKING WITH FOX COLLEAGUE AND FORMER PITTSBURGH
STEELERS QUARTERBACK TERRY BRADSHAW

"I may be dumb, but I'm not stupid."

TERRY BRADSHAW

"In other jobs, you get old, big deal. In football, you get old, you're fired. That's what happened to me. Time got me. Damned time."

LOS ANGELES RAMS HALL OF FAME DEFENSIVE END
DEACON JONES

"For a while you're a veteran, and then you're just old."

SAN DIEGO CHARGERS RECEIVER **LANCE ALWORTH**

"The older you get, the faster you ran when you were a kid."

NEW YORK GIANTS COACH **STEVE OWEN**

"I've got one advantage – when you're as slow as I am, you don't lose any steps as you grow older."

MIAMI DOLPHINS VETERAN RECEIVER **HOWARD TWILLEY**

"We professional athletes are very lucky. Unlike most mortals, we are given the privilege of dying twice – once when we retire and again when death takes us."

GREEN BAY PACKERS HALFBACK **JOHNNY (BLOOD) McNALLY**

"I knew it was time to quit when I was chewing out an official and he walked off the penalty faster than I could keep up with him."

CHICAGO BEARS OWNER AND COACH **GEORGE HALAS**, ON WHY HE GAVE UP COACHING

"I was able to push the pain down, lock it in until the game was over. I didn't know it then, but pain would be with me the rest of my life. Toward the end of my career, my joints hurt so much on Monday morning after a game that I would sometimes have to crawl from bed to the bathroom."

CHICAGO BEARS LINEBACKER DICK BUTKUS

"We had no painkillers in those days. Nothing. You lived with pain. I don't think there was ever a ballgame that most of us didn't live with pain. But you were so wrought-up playing the game that you didn't think about it. Outside of getting a little rest now and then, the one and only time I ever left a game was when Bronko Nagurski put seven stitches in my face. They took me down to the emergency room of the hospital and put the stitches in, and they brought me back in a taxicab and I went back into the ballgame."

GREEN BAY PACKERS FULLBACK CLARKE HINKLE

"In this game all you need is speed, strength and an ability to recognize pain immediately."

CINCINNATI BENGALS LINEBACKER REGGIE WILLIAMS

"Pain is only temporary,
no matter how long it lasts."

BALTIMORE RAVENS LINEBACKER **RAY LEWIS**

"I expected difficulties. This isn't earth-shattering. This isn't Hurricane Katrina."

BUFFALO BILLS GENERAL MANAGER MARV LEVY, ON THE RESIGNATION OF HEAD COACH MIKE MULARKEY JUST EIGHT DAYS AFTER THE 80-YEAR-OLD LEVY HAD TAKEN THE JOB

"You don't take yourself too seriously when you're winning, and you don't beat yourself up when you lose some games."

PITTSBURGH STEELERS COACH BILL COWHER

"Pro football gave me a good perspective. When I entered the political arena, I had already been booed, cheered, cut, sold, traded, and hung in effigy."

BUFFALO BILLS QUARTERBACK TURNED U.S. CONGRESSMAN JACK KEMP

"The world doesn't stop turning. Eventually your time runs out."

MIAMI DOLPHIN GUS FREROTTE, ON HELPING TO PREPARE A YOUNG QUARTERBACK TO TAKE HIS JOB ONE DAY

"If Marc Bulger throws an interception in Sun Devil Stadium and nobody is there to see it, is it still an interception?"

ST. LOUIS POST-DISPATCH WRITER JEFF GORDON, ON THE POOR ATTENDANCE AT ARIZONA CARDINALS GAMES

" If 'ifs' and 'buts' were candy and nuts, wouldn't it be a Merry Christmas."

DALLAS COWBOYS QUARTERBACK TURNED TV COMMENTATOR DON MEREDITH

"Old place-kickers never die, they just go on missing the point."

HALL OF FAME KICKER LOU (THE TOE) GROZA

"It's like when you have three wheels for a bike and you only need two. One has to lean against the wall. Well, here I am."

WASHINGTON REDSKINS QUARTERBACK JOE THEISMANN, ON GOING FROM A STARTER WITH THE CFL'S TORONTO ARGONAUTS TO THIRD STRING IN THE NFL

"It is better to be devoured by lions than to be eaten by dogs."

NORTHWESTERN UNIVERSITY FOOTBALL COACH
ALEX AGASE, EXPLAINING WHY HIS TEAMS PLAYED
DIFFICULT SCHEDULES

"When it rains it pours. All you can do is put your buckets out in the house when it's leaking and try to do the best you can."

CAROLINA PANTHERS RECEIVER **STEVE SMITH**, ON HIS
TEAM'S TOUGH TIME AGAINST SEATTLE IN THE 2006 NFC
CHAMPIONSHIP

"What's one more torpedo in a sinking ship?"

GREEN BAY PACKERS QUARTERBACK **LYNN DICKEY**, WHEN
ASKED WHY HE WAS STILL PLAYING FOOTBALL AFTER
HAVING SUFFERED A DISLOCATED HIPBONE, SHATTERED
HIP SOCKET, BROKEN FIBULA, AND A VARIETY OF OTHER
INJURIES

"Football kickers are like taxicabs. You can always go out and hire another one."

CHICAGO BEARS DEFENSIVE COACH **BUDDY RYAN**

For me, winning isn't something that happens suddenly on the field when the whistle blows and the crowds roar. Winning is something that builds physically and mentally every day that you train and every night that you dream.

DALLAS COWBOYS RUNNING BACK EMMITT SMITH

"Always have a plan and believe in it. I tell my coaches not to compromise. Nothing good happens by accident."

SEATTLE SEAHAWKS COACH **CHUCK KNOX**

"I am not a miracle worker. I have no magic formula. The only way I know is hard work."

DON SHULA TO THE PRESS WHEN HE WAS INTRODUCED AS COACH OF THE 3-10-1 MIAMI DOLPHINS

"You can't go out and practice average on Wednesday, average on Thursday, okay on Friday and then expect to play well on Sunday."

NEW ENGLAND PATRIOTS QUARTERBACK **TOM BRADY**

"In practice, I run every play like I'm scoring a touchdown."

MIAMI DOLPHINS RUNNING BACK **MERCURY MORRIS**

"The minute you think you've got it made, disaster is just around the corner."

PENN STATE COACH **JOE PATERNO**

"Frank Leahy was here for three years and went to war. I think sometimes that would be a welcome relief to get away from the pressures."

LOU HOLTZ, ON THE PRESSURE OF COACHING AT NOTRE DAME

"Most train to be part of the game. The greatest train to be the game: I am the game. Third-and-9, two minutes left, that's what I train for. I train for moments everyone runs from. I run to them."

DALLAS COWBOYS RECEIVER MICHAEL IRVIN

"I think you always have to re-prove. You always need to be there and rebuild that trust every game."

SEATTLE SEAHAWKS KICKER JOSH BROWN, ON THE PRESSURE OF HIS JOB

"You make a big kick, they love you. You miss a big kick, everyone wants you out."

PITTSBURGH STEELERS KICKER JEFF REED

"Pressure is something you feel when you don't know what the hell you're doing."

INDIANAPOLIS COLTS QUARTERBACK PEYTON MANNING

"Being a leader, having total control of your team, is the one asset a quarterback must have. A coach would like a skilled play caller, a slick ball handler, and an accurate passer, but one thing that is a must is having a person who can control any situation he is presented with."

GREEN BAY PACKERS COACH VINCE LOMBARDI

"I like to just sit and watch him."

CHICAGO BEARS QUARTERBACK SID LUCKMAN, ON HIS
WASHINGTON REDSKINS RIVAL SAMMY BAUGH

"Johnny Unitas is the greatest quarterback ever to play the game, better than I was, better than Sammy Baugh, better than anyone."

CHICAGO BEARS QUARTERBACK SID LUCKMAN

"In his worst games, Baugh is as good as most quarterbacks on their best days."

FOOTBALL HISTORIAN ROGER TREAT, ON WASHINGTON
REDSKINS QUARTERBACK SAMMY BAUGH

"We had a young quarterback who didn't play young. When you're around Ben, he's much more mature than his age would indicate."

PITTSBURGH STEELERS COACH **BILL COWHER**, ON QB BEN ROETHLISBERGER'S PERFORMANCE IN THE 2006 AFC CHAMPIONSHIP

"You hear about how many fourth quarter come-backs that a guy has and I think it means a guy screwed up in the first three quarters."

INDIANAPOLIS COLTS QUARTERBACK **PEYTON MANNING**

"Sometimes a guy's just a normal guy, but he's got a Microsoft brain."

SAN FRANCISCO 49ERS CORNERBACK **RONNIE LOTT**,
ON QUARTERBACK JOE MONTANA

"Anybody who ranks somebody over him, well, I just don't know where their handicapping is."

PITTSBURGH STEELERS OWNER **ART ROONEY**,
ON QUARTERBACK TERRY BRADSHAW

"You could beat Bradshaw half to death, but there'd still be enough life in him to kill you."

WASHINGTON REDSKINS COACH **GEORGE ALLEN**, ON
PITTSBURGH STEELERS QUARTERBACK TERRY BRADSHAW

"Bart's big thing was knowing what he had to do and how to do it. When he called the play, there were no doubters in the huddle."

GREEN BAY PACKERS OFFENSIVE TACKLE **FORREST GREGG**, ON QUARTERBACK BART STARR

"**A quarterback hasn't arrived until he can tell the coach to go to hell.**"

BALTIMORE COLTS QUARTERBACK **JOHNNY UNITAS**

"Coach Landry wasn't happy with my scrambling, then or ever. It was a running feud. I put up with his play-calling and he put up with my scrambling."

DALLAS COWBOYS HALL OF FAME QUARTERBACK **ROGER STAUBACH**, ON HIS RELATIONSHIP WITH COACH TOM LANDRY

"It's like getting money from home without writing."

ATLANTA FALCONS COACH **NORM VAN BROCKLIN**, ON THE SCRAMBLING ABILITY OF QUARTERBACK BOB LEE

"I couldn't believe that he'd just waste a play like that. I guess he was mad. You have to have respect for a guy like that."

BALTIMORE COLTS DEFENSIVE LINEMAN ART DONOVAN, AFTER RAMS QUARTERBACK NORM VAN BROCKLIN DELIBERATELY THREW A PASS AS HARD AS HE COULD RIGHT INTO HIS FACE

"No one ever saw John Unitas sliding into the grass after a scramble to avoid being tackled. Quarterbacks who did that were automatically labeled a sissy."

BALTIMORE COLTS DEFENSIVE LINEMAN ART DONOVAN

"I kind of don't like grades. We got a W and that's all that matters."

DENVER BRONCOS QUARTERBACK JAKE PLUMMER, ON CRITICISM OF HIS PLAY

"Roger just knew he could win in that type of situation. There was something in him that brought out his best when everything seemed hopeless."

DALLAS COWBOYS COACH TOM LANDRY, ON QUARTERBACK ROGER STAUBACH'S ABILITY TO WIN GAMES WITH LATE RALLIES

"Tom has a real good personality for a quarterback. He is confident but he is not cocky. He is assertive, but he is not overbearing."

NEW ENGLAND PATRIOTS COACH BILL BELICHICK, ON ROOKIE QUARTERBACK TOM BRADY

"There's no great mystery to quarterbacking. You move personnel around in various formations, looking for the defense's particular patsy, and then you eat him alive."

MIAMI DOLPHINS QUARTERBACK BOB GRIESE

"He can't run, he can't pass, and he can't kick – all he can do is beat you."

UNIVERSITY OF ALABAMA FOOTBALL COACH PAUL (BEAR) BRYANT, ON CRIMSON TIDE QUARTERBACK PAT TRAMMEL

"This ring is a symbol of 42 years of waiting to be a part of this."

NEW ENGLAND PATRIOTS OWNER **ROBERT KRAFT**, AFTER THE TEAM'S FIRST SUPER BOWL VICTORY

"I didn't get the ring, but I did get the Super Bowl pay bonus. I was happy about that. I'll take the bonus over the ring any day."

NEW ENGLAND PATRIOTS RESERVE TIGHT END **ZERON FLEMISTER**, WHO MISSED THE ENTIRE 2004 SEASON WITH A TORN ACHILLES TENDON

"You can go to the bank and borrow money, but you can't go to the bank and borrow a Super Bowl ring."

PITTSBURGH STEELERS DEFENSIVE LINEMAN **MEAN JOE GREENE**

"I don't wear those rings. They're too big and they catch on things."

PITTSBURGH STEELERS CHAIRMAN **DAN ROONEY**, ON HIS FIVE SUPER BOWL RINGS

"We never got a ring for winning. We got a nine-dollar blue blanket that said, 'World Champions.'"

FORMER DETROIT LIONS QUARTERBACK **BOBBY LAYNE**, ON WINNING THE 1952 NFL TITLE

"He was most dangerous when you thought you had him. He'd gather himself up and you'd find your-self empty-handed."

NEW YORK GIANTS LINEBACKER SAM HUFF, ON LEGENDARY CLEVELAND BROWNS RUNNING BACK JIM BROWN

"He looks no different than any other runner when he's coming at you, but when he gets there, he's gone."

SAN FRANCISCO 49ERS DEFENSIVE BACK GEORGE DONNELLY, ON CHICAGO BEARS RUNNING BACK GALE SAYERS

"He was an artful dodger drilled and practiced in the techniques of avoiding tacklers skilled in the employment of every artifice of mental and physi-cal razzle-dazzle and bafflement."

SPORTSWRITER PAUL GALLICO, ON FOOTBALL LEGEND RED GRANGE

"Franco Harris faked me out so bad one time that I got a 15-yard penalty for grabbing my own face mask."

TAMPA BAY BUCCANEERS LINEBACKER DAVID LEWIS

"Has the feet of a tap dancer."

SCOUTING REPORT ON MIAMI DOLPHINS RUNNING BACK
MERCURY MORRIS

"He moves almost with no effort as a shadow flits
and drifts and darts."

LEGENDARY SPORTSWRITER GRANTLAND RICE, ON
FOOTBALL IMMORTAL RED GRANGE, KNOWN AS "THE
GALLOPING GHOST"

"You've heard of people who zig or zag. Well, Elroy Hirsch also had a zog and a couple of zugs."

FORMER LOS ANGELES RAMS QUARTERBACK
NORM VAN BROCKLIN, ON HIS FELLOW HALL OF FAME
TEAMMATE, WHO WAS KNOWN AS "CRAZY LEGS"

"A lot of fans were drawn to me because they knew
that whatever the score was, I was going to run as
hard as I could on every play. You don't have that
now; you have guys waiting for next week or even
next year."

CHICAGO BEARS RUNNING BACK WALTER PAYTON

It's probably
similar to being
in New York City
and having a
cabdriver behind
you and you're driving too slow.
It's not the most pleasant thing.

DETROIT LIONS RUNNING BACK **BARRY SANDERS**,
ON WHAT IT MUST HAVE BEEN LIKE TO PLAY AGAINST HIM

"You need two yards, I'll get you three. You need 10 yards, I'll get you three."

RUNNING BACK LEROY HOARD, WHO AVERAGED 3.9 YARDS PER CARRY OVER A TEN-YEAR CAREER WITH FOUR DIFFERENT TEAMS

"There were a lot of running backs as good as me. The real difference was that I could focus. I never laid back and relied on natural ability."

LEGENDARY CLEVELAND BROWNS RUNNING BACK JIM BROWN

"Football goes in cycles. Wide ties keep coming back again. So will the running game."

NEW ORLEANS SAINTS QUARTERBACK ARCHIE MANNING (FATHER OF PEYTON AND ELI), ON THE NFL IN THE EARLY 1980s

"You don't get hurt running straight ahead ... three-yards-and-a-cloud-of-dust offense. I will pound you and pound you until you quit."

OHIO STATE FOOTBALL COACH WOODY HAYES

"The forward pass has brought in so many compli-cated rules in the U.S. that much of their best ball-carrying is now done by the referees."

PLAYER, COACH AND SPORTSWRITER TED REEVES, ON THE INTRODUCTION OF FORWARD PASSING TO FOOTBALL IN EASTERN CANADA IN 1931

"Only three things can happen when you put a ball up in the air – and two of them are bad."

MICHIGAN STATE FOOTBALL COACH DUFFY DAUGHERTY

"We started throwing the ball well last year. If we can catch it this year, we should be OK."

ST. LOUIS HIGH FOOTBALL COACH **RON MARCIEL**

"Football is nothing more than a series of actions, mistakes, and miscalculations. Punt and make your opposition make the mistakes."

UNIVERSITY OF TENNESSEE FOOTBALL COACH
BOB NEYLAND

"When in doubt, punt."

LEGENDARY COLLEGE FOOTBALL COACH **JOHN HEISMAN**

"I don't know how drastic it is. That's up to people who measure drastic-ticity, or whatever the word is. Drastic-ticians."

TAMPA BAY BUCCANEERS COACH JON GRUDEN, ON THE TEAM GOING FROM WORST TO FIRST IN THE NFC SOUTH DIVISION IN 2005

"We've got to keep it in retrospective."

BUFFALO BILLS QUARTERBACK JIM KELLY, WHOSE TEAM LOST THE SUPER BOWL FOUR YEARS IN A ROW

"The only way to describe him was 'indescribable.'"

UNIVERSITY OF TENNESSEE HEAD COACH BILL BATTLE, ON QUARTERBACK CONDREDGE HOLLOWAY

"I've always said the sun doesn't shine on the same dog every day, but we sure as heck didn't expect a near total eclipse."

TEXAS TECH COACH STEVE SLOAN, AFTER HIS UNDEFEATED TEAM BARELY BEAT WINLESS TEXAS CHRISTIAN

"I knew I'd bounce back. I wasn't dead or anything."

SEATTLE SEAHAWKS RECEIVER DARRELL JACKSON, ON THE CONCUSSION HE SUFFERED DURING THE 2002 SEASON

"From the waist down, Earl Campbell has the biggest legs I have ever seen on a running back."

"If I drop dead tomorrow, at least I'll know I died in good health."

HOUSTON OILERS COACH BUM PHILLIPS, AFTER PASSING A PHYSICAL

"I'm very appreciative of being indicted."

FORMER FLORIDA STATE COACH BILL PETERSON, ON BEING INDUCTED INTO THE FLORIDA SPORTS HALL OF FAME

"He had a small window, but he hit the middle of the bull's-eye."

PITTSBURGH STEELERS RECEIVER HINES WARD, ON A TOUCHDOWN PASS THROWN BY QUARTERBACK BEN ROETHLISBERGER

"I was always coming back unless I said I wasn't."

INDIANAPOLIS COLTS COACH TONY DUNGY, ANNOUNCING HE PLANNED TO RETURN AFTER CONTEMPLATING RETIREMENT FOLLOWING THE 2005 SEASON

"If I went to a team that already had a starter, then I'd have to be a backup."

NEW YORK JETS QUARTERBACK CHAD PENNINGTON, ON WHY HE RE-SIGNED WITH THE TEAM

"When you're not done, you're not done. It's a hard feeling to describe."

FORMER UNIVERSITY OF NEBRASKA QUARTERBACK
ERIC CROUCH, WHO WON THE HEISMAN TROPHY IN 2001,
HOPING TO RESTART HIS CAREER WITH THE TORONTO
ARGONAUTS IN 2006

"He treats us like men. He lets us wear earrings."

UNIVERSITY OF HOUSTON RECEIVER TORRIN POLK,
ON COACH JOHN JENKINS

"I want to rush for 1,000 or 1,500 yards, whichever comes first."

NEW ORLEANS SAINTS RUNNING BACK GEORGE ROGERS,
ON HIS GOALS FOR THE UPCOMING SEASON

"New names don't scare nobody."

NEW YORK GIANTS DEFENSIVE BACK ERICH BARNES

"He's the kind of player who usually comes along rarely and sometimes never."

MINNESOTA VIKINGS COACH BUD GRANT, ON DEFENSIVE
TACKLE ALAN PAGE

"It's a once-in-a-lifetime thing that only happens every so often."

MINNESOTA VIKINGS RECEIVER RANDY MOSS, ON HIS
NO-LOOK, OVER-THE-SHOULDER LATERAL TO MOE
WILLIAMS FOR A 59-YARD TOUCHDOWN

"I've been big ever since I was little."

CHICAGO BEARS DEFENSIVE LINEMAN
WILLIAM (THE REFRIGERATOR) PERRY

"Probably the Beatles' *White Album*."

> SEATTLE SEAHAWK STEVE LARGENT, ONCE THE NFL'S
> ALL-TIME LEADER IN SIX CATEGORIES, INCLUDING
> RECEPTIONS AND RECEIVING YARDS, WHEN ASKED
> WHICH RECORD HE TREASURED MOST

"I can't even count to 10 in English."

> PITTSBURGH STEELERS RECEIVER LEE MAYS, WHEN ASKED
> BEFORE SUPER BOWL XL IF HE COULD COUNT TO 10 IN A
> FOREIGN LANGUAGE

"The Cowboys won the Super Bowl last season, and I didn't see them graduating any seniors."

> PHILADELPHIA EAGLES COACH DICK VERMEIL, ON WHY
> DALLAS WAS THE FAVORITE IN 1978

"It's kind of like comparing the Atlantic and Pacific oceans. They'll both drown you."

> KANSAS STATE COACH JIM DICKEY, WHEN ASKED TO
> COMPARE THE OKLAHOMA SOONERS OF 1978 WITH THE
> 1977 TEAM

"Kansas State hasn't won a Big Eight championship in 40 years. I told them that if I don't win one in that same length of time, I'll resign."

> KANSAS STATE COACH JIM DICKEY

"**I've been a quarterback since high school. I've always been black.**"

WASHINGTON REDSKIN **DOUG WILLIAMS**, ANSWERING THE QUESTION, "HOW LONG HAVE YOU BEEN A BLACK QUARTERBACK?"

"It's all right by me as long as all of them do it, and not just two of them."

KANSAS CITY CHIEFS COACH PAUL WIGGINS, ON PLAYERS HOLDING HANDS IN THE HUDDLE

"Rapport? You mean like, 'You run as fast as you can, and I'll throw it as far as I can'?"

SAN FRANCISCO 49ERS QUARTERBACK JEFF KEMP WHEN ASKED ABOUT HIS RAPPORT WITH WIDE RECEIVER JERRY RICE

"They sure have a lot of turnovers. Every time you look around, they're kicking off."

INDIANA COACH LEE CORSO, WHEN ASKED IF MICHIGAN HAD ANY WEAKNESSES

"It could have been a lot worse. We could have been killed in a car crash driving home."

MIAMI DOLPHINS QUARTERBACK BOB GRIESE, AFTER
BREAKING HIS LEG EARLY IN THE TEAM'S PERFECT SEASON
OF 1972

"I don't know. I haven't tried it. Maybe last year was."

WASHINGTON REDSKINS QUARTERBACK SAMMY BAUGH,
RESPONDING TO THE QUESTION, "IS THIS YOUR LAST
SEASON?"

"I don't know. We'll find out soon."

VANDERBILT QUARTERBACK JAY CUTLER, A POSSIBLE #1
PICK IN THE 2006 NFL DRAFT, WHEN ASKED IF A CONTRACT
WORTH MILLIONS OF DOLLARS WOULD CHANGE HIM

"I just recall a loss as long as it takes to learn why we lost it."

MIAMI DOLPHINS QUARTERBACK **BOB GRIESE**

"I've always played with a sense of urgency since my rookie year and I've never accepted losing. I never like to say, 'That's okay, we'll get them next year,' because it's not okay."

INDIANAPOLIS COLTS QUARTERBACK **PEYTON MANNING**, AFTER THE TEAM'S 14-2 SEASON IN 2005 ENDED WITH A DISAPPOINTING PLAYOFF LOSS TO PITTSBURGH

"When you lose, you want to go down fighting, you want to go down playing your best, and we didn't do that."

NEW ENGLAND PATRIOTS QUARTERBACK **TOM BRADY**, AFTER A DISAPPOINTING PLAYOFF LOSS TO DENVER ENDED THE TEAM'S CHANCES AT WINNING THREE STRAIGHT SUPER BOWLS

"There never was a champion who to himself was a good loser. There's a vast difference between a good sport and a good loser."

ARMY FOOTBALL COACH **RED BLAIK**

"**Statistics are a salve. You rub them on your wounds after you lose and you feel a little better.**"

CINCINNATI BENGALS COACH **BILL (TIGER) JOHNSON**

"I love football. I think it is the most wonderful game in the world and I despise to lose."

OHIO STATE FOOTBALL COACH **WOODY HAYES**

"If you can accept defeat and open your pay envelope without feeling guilty, you're stealing."

WASHINGTON REDSKINS COACH **GEORGE ALLEN**

"It was a brain transplant. I got a sportswriter's brain so I could be sure I had one that hadn't been used."

MINNESOTA VIKINGS COACH **NORM VAN BROCKLIN**, WHEN ASKED ABOUT A RECENT OPERATION

"**What's the difference between a three-week-old puppy and a sportswriter? In six weeks, the puppy stops whining.**"

CHICAGO BEARS COACH **MIKE DITKA**

"No man, I majored in Journalism. It was easier."

NEW YORK JETS QUARTERBACK **JOE NAMATH**, RESPONDING TO A JOURNALIST WHO ASKED HIM IF HE MAJORED IN BASKET WEAVING AT ALABAMA

"Having two weeks off gives family, friends and the media more time to get on your nerves."

DALLAS COWBOYS DEFENSIVE BACK **DEION SANDERS**, ON WHY HE DOESN'T LIKE THE TWO-WEEK BREAK BETWEEN THE CONFERENCE CHAMPIONSHIP AND THE SUPER BOWL

"It's doubtful any of them would object if the game were being played in a mall parking lot in Anchorage, Alaska."

SOUTH FLORIDA SUN-SENTINEL COLUMNIST
CHARLES BRICKER, ON THE FACT THAT SEATTLE WAS
MAKING ITS FIRST SUPER BOWL APPEARANCE IN DETROIT
RATHER THAN IN A WARM WEATHER VACATION SPOT

"Every kid dreams of doing this. I'm getting an opportunity to live a dream."

PITTSBURGH STEELERS QUARTERBACK
BEN ROETHLISBERGER, ON PLAYING IN THE SUPER BOWL

"This is what it's all about. Seventeen and o says it all."

MIAMI DOLPHINS COACH DON SHULA, AFTER VICTORY IN
SUPER BOWL VII CAPPED THE TEAM'S PERFECT SEASON

"Before the Super Bowl game, both teams are treated equally. And when it's over, there's only one team in the land. The other is forgotten."

MIAMI DOLPHINS COACH DON SHULA

"The things you do individually are great, but the reason you play this game is to win the championship."

PITTSBURGH STEELERS RUNNING BACK JEROME BETTIS, WHO ANNOUNCED HIS RETIREMENT AFTER PITTSBURGH WON SUPER BOWL XL

"Do you know what happens after you lose the Super Bowl? The world ends. It just stops."

MINNESOTA VIKINGS QUARTERBACK JOE KAPP

"If it's the ultimate game, how come they're playing it again next year?"

DALLAS COWBOYS RUNNING BACK DUANE THOMAS AT SUPER BOWL VI

"His father gave him a six-week-old puppy when he was four, and he traded it away for two twelve-year-old cats."

WASHINGTON REDSKINS PRESIDENT EDWARD BENNETT WILLIAMS ON COACH GEORGE ALLEN, WHO ALWAYS PREFERRED VETERAN PLAYERS

"Aren't you a little old for this sort of thing?"

39-YEAR-OLD BALTIMORE COLTS QUARTERBACK JOHNNY UNITAS, TO 38-YEAR-OLD FORMER TEAMMATE EARL MORRALL OF MIAMI

"I'm old enough to know my limitations and I'm young enough to exceed them."

BUFFALO BILLS GENERAL MANGER MARV LEVY, ON BEING HIRED FOR THE JOB AT AGE 80

"What he's doing, it shouldn't happen. I marvel at him. He's amazing."

CFL LEGEND RON LANCASTER, ON TORONTO ARGONAUTS QUARTERBACK DAMON ALLEN (BROTHER OF MARCUS ALLEN), WHO HAS PASSED LANCASTER AS THE CFL'S ALL-TIME PASSING LEADER AND WAS LEAGUE MVP FOR THE FIRST TIME AT AGE 42

"I have to keep playing so people over **40** will have somebody to root for on Sunday afternoons."

OAKLAND RAIDERS QUARTERBACK/KICKER GEORGE BLANDA, WHO PLAYED UNTIL HE WAS 46

"When I turned 40, this team took a chance on me. The oldest franchise in the league traded for the oldest quarterback in the league, so I always felt that it was a match made in heaven."

ALL-TIME CFL PASSING LEADER DAMON ALLEN, ON SIGNING WITH THE TORONTO ARGONAUTS (FORMED IN 1874)

"They say two things happen when you get older. One is you begin to forget things, and I can't remember what the other thing is."

80-YEAR-OLD BUFFALO BILLS GENERAL MANAGER MARV LEVY

"Pass the Maalox and full-speed ahead."

TORONTO STAR COLUMNIST RICHARD GRIFFIN, ON THE BUFFALO BILLS' TRIUMVIRATE OF 87-YEAR-OLD OWNER RALPH WILSON, 80-YEAR-OLD GM MARV LEVY AND 55-YEAR-OLD COACH DICK JAURON

"When the going gets tough, the tough get going."

UNIVERSITY OF ALABAMA FOOTBALL COACH
PAUL (BEAR) BRYANT. (THIS QUOTE IS ATTRIBUTED TO
MANY, BUT WAS PROBABLY ORIGINATED BY BRYANT.)

"Training camp is tough, and there's some pain. But it's a good life. It's better than working."

CHICAGO BEARS DEFENSIVE END DOUG ATKINS

"In the 1950s, the players were tougher because they came out of World War II. We had a different mentality. We were raised to love your God, respect your elders, and fear no son-of-a-bitch that walks. It was survival of the fittest."

PHILADELPHIA EAGLES DEFENSIVE LINEMAN
BUCKO KILROY

"I'm not trying to win a popularity poll. I'm trying to win football games. I don't like nice people. I like tough, honest people."

OHIO STATE FOOTBALL COACH WOODY HAYES

"There's no tougher way to make easy money than pro football."

HALL OF FAME QUARTERBACK AND COACH **NORM VAN BROCKLIN**

"I don't care how much talent a team has – if the boys don't think tough, practice tough, and live tough, how can they play tough on Saturday?"

UNIVERSITY OF ALABAMA FOOTBALL COACH
PAUL (BEAR) BRYANT

"All I know is that we went out there in two buses and we came back in one."

FORMER TEXAS A&M PLAYER AND ALABAMA FOOTBALL
COACH GENE STALLINGS, WHEN ASKED IF COACH BEAR
BRYANT'S PRACTICES WERE AS TOUGH AS REPORTED

"They don't want to play smash-mouth football. They want to trick you."

PITTSBURGH STEELERS LINEBACKER JOEY PORTER, ON THE INDIANAPOLIS COLTS, WHOM THE STEELERS BEAT EN ROUTE TO SUPER BOWL XL

"Don't say anything to Steve. If you don't say anything, it kind of confuses him. Once you start talking trash, he will make it a point to embarrass you."

DETROIT LIONS RECEIVERS COACH FRED GRAVES, ON CAROLINA PANTHERS RECEIVER STEVE SMITH, WHOM HE COACHED IN COLLEGE AT UTAH

"He couldn't spell 'cat' if you spotted him the C and the A."

DALLAS COWBOYS LINEBACKER THOMAS (HOLLYWOOD) HENDERSON, TAKING A SHOT AT THE INTELLIGENCE OF PITTSBURGH STEELERS QUARTERBACK TERRY BRADSHAW PRIOR TO SUPER BOWL XIII

"Empty barrels make the most noise."

PITTSBURGH STEELERS COACH CHUCK NOLL, REACTING TO THOMAS HENDERSON'S SHOT AT TERRY BRADSHAW

"When my mouth is running, my motor is running. If I was mute, I couldn't play this game. I put a lot of pressure on myself to see if I can play up to my mouth."

DALLAS COWBOYS LINEBACKER
THOMAS (HOLLYWOOD) HENDERSON

"My father taught me never to interrupt."

LEGENDARY NOTRE DAME FOOTBALL COACH
KNUTE ROCKNE, ON WHY HE COULDN'T SWAP REMARKS
WITH MICHIGAN COACH FIELDING YOST

"Never overload your butt with your mouth."

SEATTLE SEAHAWKS COACH CHUCK KNOX

"If we'd listened to the experts, we shouldn't even bothered showing up."

NEW ENGLAND PATRIOTS DEFENSIVE LINEMAN
WILLIE McGINEST, ON THE TEAM'S UPSET OF THE ST. LOUIS
RAMS IN SUPER BOWL XXXVI

"We're always going to be the other team. We win 11 in a row and they say it's our fault the other teams weren't as good."

SEATTLE SEAHAWKS RUNNING BACK **SHAUN ALEXANDER**,
ON HIS TEAM'S LACK OF MEDIA ATTENTION IN 2005

"I don't think anyone is picking us to win. Obviously, they're the best team in football. We're just going to go in and obviously try to find a way to just put a few points on the board."

PITTSBURGH STEELERS QUARTERBACK
BEN ROETHLISBERGER, ON HIS TEAM'S CHANCES
AGAINST THE 14-2 INDIANAPOLIS COLTS IN THEIR
2006 AFC PLAYOFF GAME. THE STEELERS WON.

"We'll waffle them."

HAMILTON TIGER-CATS COACH **JIM TRIMBLE**, ON WHAT
HIS TEAM WOULD DO TO WINNIPEG IN THE 1958 GREY CUP.
THEY DIDN'T. THE BLUE BOMBERS WON 35-28

"There is simply no way we can beat Notre Dame. But Notre Dame could lose to us."

GEORGIA TECH COACH **PEPPER RODGERS**

"It will take an act of God to beat us."

TORONTO ARGONAUTS COACH **LEO CAHILL** BEFORE A PLAYOFF GAME WITH THE OTTAWA ROUGH RIDERS. AFTER OVERNIGHT RAIN AND A HARD FROST, THE ARGOS LOST 32-3.

"A lot of people told him the world was flat, but he kept going until he found land."

PITTSBURGH STEELERS COACH **BILL COWHER**, COMPARING HIS TEAM'S DIFFICULT ROAD TO VICTORY IN SUPER BOWL XL TO CHRISTOPHER COLUMBUS' VOYAGE TO THE NEW WORLD

"We took the scenic route."

PITTSBURGH STEELERS LINEBACKER **JOEY PORTER**, ON THE TEAM'S DIFFICULT ROAD TO THE CHAMPIONSHIP AT SUPER BOWL XL

"Winning isn't everything, but it beats anything that comes in second."

UNIVERSITY OF ALABAMA FOOTBALL COACH
PAUL (BEAR) BRYANT

"Go out that door – to victory!"

CLIMAX TO A LEGENDARY HALFTIME SPEECH DELIVERED BY
LEGENDARY UNIVERSITY OF MICHIGAN FOOTBALL COACH
FIELDING YOST

"There isn't anything wrong with winning ugly. As a matter of fact, there isn't anything wrong with being ugly – as long as you're successful."

COLLEGE FOOTBALL COACH **LOU HOLTZ**

"We've got to find a way to win. I'm willing to start cheating."

NEW ENGLAND PATRIOTS TIGHT END **MARV COOK**

"Just as long as the team wins, it doesn't matter who gets the glory. If I can make a contribution catching the ball or blocking, as long as we win, that's the most important thing."

MIAMI DOLPHINS RECEIVER **PAUL WARFIELD**, DURING THE
TEAM'S PERFECT SEASON IN 1972

"Winning isn't everything; it's the only thing."

LEGENDARY GREEN BAY PACKERS COACH VINCE LOMBARDI

"Every time you win, you're reborn. When you lose, you die a little."

WASHINGTON REDSKINS COACH GEORGE ALLEN

"A tie is like kissing your sister."

MICHIGAN STATE FOOTBALL COACH DUFFY DAUGHERTY

"Three rules for coaching: 1) Surround yourself with people who can't live without football. 2) Recognize winners. They come in all forms. 3) Have a plan for everything."

UNIVERSITY OF ALABAMA FOOTBALL COACH
PAUL (BEAR) BRYANT

"Nothing is work unless you'd rather be doing something else."

CHICAGO BEARS FOUNDER, OWNER AND COACH
GEORGE HALAS

"I'm fairly confident that if I died tomorrow, Don would find a way to preserve me until the season was over and he had time for a nice funeral."

DOROTHY SHULA, ON THE CAREER DEDICATION OF HER
HUSBAND, MIAMI DOLPHINS COACH DON SHULA

"What royal wedding?"

PHILADELPHIA EAGLES COACH DICK VERMEIL, WHEN
ASKED IF HE PLANNED TO WATCH THE ROYAL WEDDING OF
PRINCE CHARLES AND LADY DIANA

"There are no office hours for champions."

LOUISIANA STATE FOOTBALL COACH **PAUL DIETZEL**

Eric Zweig has written for the *Toronto Star, The Globe and Mail* and the *Toronto Sun.* He is also the author or editor of dozens of books including *Total Hockey, 99: My Life in Pictures* and *The Toronto Blue Jays Official 25th Anniversary Commemorative Book.* A third-generation football fan, he had Joe Theismann sign his cast when he was eight years old.